# FOCUS

## on Writing

# Writing

## Book 1

**John Jackman and
Wendy Wren**

**Collins**

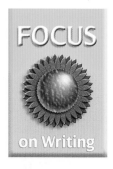

# Using this book

*This book will help you to develop your writing skills to become a really successful writer.*

## What's in a unit
Each unit is set out in the same way as the example here.

**Unit heading**
This tells you what you will be learning about

**Think about it**
Activities to practise, check and develop your writing skills

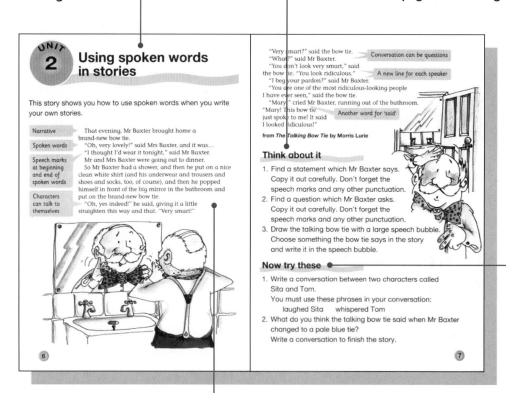

**The text**
The texts have been carefully selected to demonstrate all major genre types, from fiction to non-fiction. Annotations point out useful techniques and help you to see what really works

**Now try these**
Activities to stretch and extend your writing skills

# Contents

# Story settings

Here is a part of a longer story. It shows you how a writer can help readers imagine where and when the story is taking place.

A setting based on experience

Lots of detail helps you to imagine the setting

Marian and Simon were sent to bed early on the day that the Brown family moved house. By then everyone had lost their temper with everyone else; the cat had been sick on the sitting-room carpet; the dog had run away twice. If you have ever moved you will know what kind of a day it had been. Packing cases and newspaper all over the place ...sandwiches instead of proper meals ...the kettle lost and the wardrobe stuck on the stairs and Mrs Brown's favourite vase broken. There was bread and baked beans for supper, the television wouldn't work and the water wasn't hot so when all was said and done the children didn't object too violently to being packed off to bed. They'd had enough too. They had

one last argument about who was going to sleep by the window, put on their pyjamas, got into bed, switched the lights out...and it was at that point that the ghost came out of the bottom drawer of the chest of drawers.

> A clue to something unusual in the story

from *Uninvited Ghosts and Other Stories* by Penelope Lively

## Think about it

Use the description to draw a picture of a messy room in the Brown's house on moving day. Write labels on your picture.

Mrs Brown's favourite vase

## Now try these

1. Write a short description of your street.
2. Imagine your classroom is being moved down the hall. Write a short description of:
   a) what the classroom looks like while everything is being packed
   b) what the classroom looks like when everything has been taken away.

# Using spoken words in stories

This story shows you how to use spoken words when you write your own stories.

| | |
|---|---|
| Narrative | That evening, Mr Baxter brought home a brand-new bow tie. |
| Spoken words | "Oh, very lovely!" said Mrs Baxter, and it was… "I thought I'd wear it tonight," said Mr Baxter. |
| Speech marks at beginning and end of spoken words | Mr and Mrs Baxter were going out to dinner. So Mr Baxter had a shower, and then he put on a nice clean white shirt (and his underwear and trousers and shoes and socks, too, of course), and then he popped himself in front of the big mirror in the bathroom and put on the brand-new bow tie. |
| Characters can talk to themselves | "Oh, yes indeed!" he said, giving it a little straighten this way and that. "Very smart!" |

"Very smart?" said the bow tie.

"What?" said Mr Baxter.

"You don't look very smart," said the bow tie. "You look ridiculous."

"I beg your pardon?" said Mr Baxter.

"You are one of the most ridiculous-looking people I have ever seen," said the bow tie.

"Mary!" cried Mr Baxter, running out of the bathroom. "Mary! This bow tie just spoke to me! It said I looked ridiculous!"

*Conversation can be questions*

*A new line for each speaker*

*Another word for 'said'*

**from *The Talking Bow Tie* by Morris Lurie**

# Think about it

1. Find a statement which Mr Baxter says. Copy it out carefully. Don't forget the speech marks and any other punctuation.
2. Find a question which Mr Baxter asks. Copy it out carefully. Don't forget the speech marks and any other punctuation.
3. Draw the talking bow tie with a large speech bubble. Choose something the bow tie says in the story and write it in the speech bubble.

# Now try these

1. Write a conversation between two characters called Sita and Tom.
   You must use these phrases in your conversation:
   laughed Sita     whispered Tom
2. What do you think the talking bow tie said when Mr Baxter changed to a pale blue tie?
   Write a conversation to finish the story.

# UNIT 3 Story openings

Here are the openings of two stories. They help you learn about writing interesting beginnings.

Opening gives
the time of
year as setting

It was Christmas Eve, and Tom and Kate were very excited – over-excited, their mother said. But then Grandma and Grandpa had come to stay, and the thought of bulging stockings on Christmas morning; the Christmas tree with the parcels round it; and all those good things to eat, made it difficult to sit still.

from *When Grandma
Took a Back Seat*
by Nancy Blishen

It was on the second day of Peter's holiday with his grandmother that the Martian came to the cottage. There was a knock at the door and when he went to open it there was this small green person with webbed feet and eyes on the end of stumpy antennae who said, perfectly politely, 'I wonder if I might bother you for the loan of a spanner?'

A surprise opening

**from *Uninvited Ghosts and Other Stories* by Penelope Lively**

# Think about it

**Look at the two story openings.**

1. Which opening makes you want to read the story? Give your reasons.
2. Which opening do you think is the least interesting? Give your reasons.

# Now try these

**Write two story openings.**

1. Tell the reader what time of year it is and where your story takes place.
2. Start your story with a surprise.

# UNIT 4 Shape poems

You can use any shape you think of to write a shape poem. It's a good idea to start with a simple shape. These two are fun, but rather hard to do.

**Toothpaste**

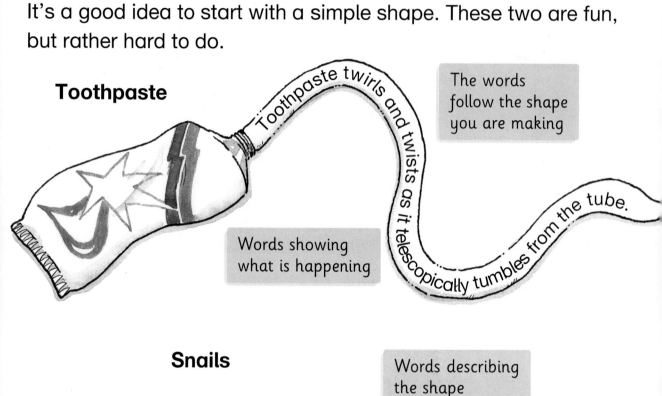

Toothpaste twirls and twists as it telescopically tumbles from the tube.

The words follow the shape you are making

Words showing what is happening

**Snails**

Words describing the shape

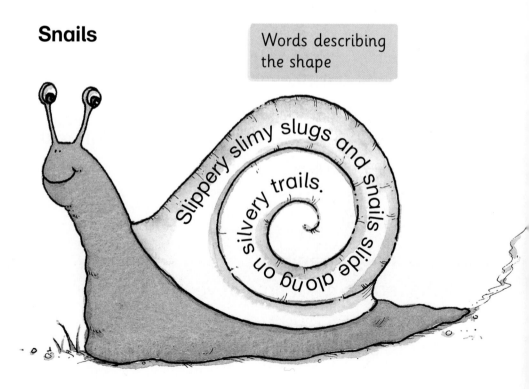

Slippery slimy slugs and snails slide along on silvery trails.

# Think about it

## Toothpaste

1. What letter does most of the words in the poem begin with?
2. Why do you think the poet chose that letter?
3. What is the poem describing?
4. What is the shape of the poem?

## Snails

1. What letter does most of the words in the poem begin with?
2. Why do you think the poet chose that letter?
3. What is the poem describing?
4. What is the shape of the poem?

# Now try these

Choose one of the following and write your own shape poem.

# Turning a story into a play

You can change a story into a play. Here is how it was done with a story called *The Digger*.

| | |
|---|---|
| **Opening with conversation and narrative** | "They're at it again!" said Daniel's Dad. |

For weeks the men had been digging at the end of the road.

"First it was the gas, and then the water, and now it's the council."

Daniel liked to watch the workmen. "I wouldn't mind digging holes in the road, and sitting in a little hut, and making tea over a fire," he said.

| | |
|---|---|
| **Narrative gives setting and tells about the characters** | But one morning he went along the road to school and there was no one there. No workmen. No one brewing tea. No one digging. Just a hole in the road. Daniel looked at the hole and wondered how deep it was. Perhaps it went down, down, down into the ground. |

| | |
|---|---|
| **The conversation is in speech marks** | "Hallo there!" said a voice. Daniel looked round, surprised. But there was no one there. |

"I'm over here," said a voice. Daniel could hardly believe his eyes. There, sitting on the edge of the pavement, was a kangaroo....."Take a good look," said the kangaroo. "You don't see many of us around here."

A real kangaroo! A talking kangaroo! Daniel just stared. Then he said,"But...but, where have you come from?"

| | |
|---|---|
| **The conversation also tells who is speaking** | "Australia," said the kangaroo in an off-hand way... |

**from *The Digger* by Anne Forsyth**

## Scene 1: In Daniel's kitchen

*Daniel and his dad are looking out of the window. There is a lot of noise coming from outside.*

**Daniel's Dad:** They're at it again! First it was the gas, and then the water, and now it's the council.

**Daniel:** I wouldn't mind digging holes in the road, and sitting in a little hut, and making tea over a fire.

Description of setting (scene)

No speech marks in play conversation

## Scene 2: Daniel on his way to school

*Daniel is going along the road where the workmen have been digging, but there is no one there now.*

**Kangaroo:** Hallo there! I'm over here.

*Daniel sees a kangaroo sitting on the edge of the pavement.*

**Kangaroo:** Take a good look. You don't see many of us around here.

**Daniel:** *Staring at the kangaroo.* But...but, where have you come from?

**Kangaroo:** *In an off-hand way.* Australia.

Stage directions tell players what to do

Name of each speaker on new line

## Think about it

1. How many characters are in the play?
2. Where is Scene 1 set?
3. Where is Scene 2 set?
4. Read the playscript and copy out one example of:
   a) where a scene is set
   b) a stage direction
   c) a character's name
   d) spoken words (dialogue)

## Now try these

1. Continue the play from where the Kangaroo tells Daniel that he comes from Australia.
   a) What does Daniel say?
   b) What happens next?
2. Choose a part of one of your favourite stories and write it as a play.

# UNIT 6 — Giving information

This page shows you one way to write an information book. There is a main heading, a picture and smaller headings to help you find the information you want.

## Machines in the home
*Main heading*

Machines can help us do jobs more easily and more quickly, but they are also dangerous if not used with great care.

*Key words*

◆ **Cooker**
This is used to cook and heat our meals. Some cookers use gas and some use electricity. A few use both gas and electricity.

*Sub-headings make it easier to find information*

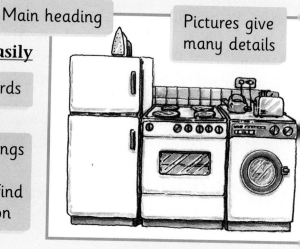

*Pictures give many details*

*Machines in the kitchen*

◆ **Electric kettle**
Inside the kettle is a wire inside a tube. This is called the element. It gets hot and heats the water inside the kettle until it boils. The outside of a kettle can get very hot.

◆ **Toaster**
A toaster has elements too. The lever on the side turns the element on, and a catch inside the toaster turns it off when the bread is toasted. Never put anything except bread in a toaster.

◆ **Fridge and freezer**
Food goes bad more quickly if it isn't kept cool. An electric motor makes the air inside a fridge cooler so the food stays fresh for a few days. In freezers the air is very cold, to make the food freeze and stay fresh for a few weeks.

◆ **Washing machine**
Electricity works the motor that turns the drum and heats the water.

◆ **Iron**
The element is inside, so a hot and cold iron look exactly the same, so never touch an iron or it may burn you badly!

# Think about it

1. Write a list of the machines in this kitchen.
2. Make a list of all the machines that your family uses inside and outside the kitchen.

# Now try these

1. Sort all the machines in your home. Make a chart like this. Some machines will be in more than one list.

| Machines that need electricity | Machines that need gas | Machines that need water | Machines that need petrol or oil |
|---|---|---|---|
|  |  |  |  |

2. Copy each of these. Next to each machine say what it is used for in not more than five words. The first one has been done for you.
   a) washing machine    cleans dirty clothes
   b) fridge
   c) vacuum cleaner
   d) power drill
   e) bike
   f) iron
3. Make a poster for young children warning them about the dangers in a kitchen.

# Writing a report

You need to tell the most important points when you write a report. Here is a report that says everything clearly.

This is what Kiran wrote after he had been on a day trip to a holiday park.

When, who and where

What was there

How the writer felt

Conclusion

On Friday 17th April our family went to Blaxland Holiday Park. We have been before, but this was the first time our cousins, Meena, Gopal and Jasmine, had come with us.

There was a huge indoor swimming pool at the centre, and equipment for lots of other sports and games. There was also a lake and go-cart track.

The thing we enjoyed most was the swimming pool because it was a very hot day, and it was fun because it had rapids, water shoots and a wave machine.

We also liked going on the pedaloes. We had a race, which Mum and Dad won!

I wish we could have had a ride on the go-carts, but it was too expensive.

It had been a really good day. We went for a pizza and coke on the way home and we were pleased when Mum and Dad said that we can have another visit in a few weeks time.

## Think about it

Think about a day trip you have had.
Write about it in the way Kiran wrote about his trip.
Copy the words Kiran used and complete
each sentence in your own words.

On … went to …
There was …
The thing we enjoyed most was …
We also liked …
I wish we could have …
It had been …

## Now try these

Write about a school visit you have made.
Use these sentences to help you.

The main reason that I found our visit to _____
interesting was that _____
We learnt that _____
The most surprising thing I discovered was _____
I am pleased I went to _____ because _____

17

# A story plan

This is a plan for writing a story. It can be used to decide who the characters are and what they do at the beginning of the story, then in the middle and end of the story.

**Daedelus and Icarus**

| | |
|---|---|
| Beginning | King Minos captured the Minotaur. |
| Decide on setting and opening | He asked Daedelus to make a labyrinth to imprison the Minotaur. |
| Decide how many characters | Daedelus wanted to leave Crete with his son Icarus after he finished the job. |
| Middle | King Minos wouldn't let them leave and put them in a high tower. |
| Write some conversation | Daedelus made wings of birds' feathers stuck together with wax for Icarus to escape. |
| Describe important parts | Daedelus told Icarus not to fly too high or the sun would melt the wax. |
| End | Icarus flew too close to the sun and the wings came apart. He fell into the sea and died. |

Decide ending before starting to write

## Think about it

1. In your own words write:
    a) What happened at the beginning of the story.
    b) What happened in the middle of the story.
    c) What happened at the end of the story.
2. Draw and write about one of the scenes (setting) you would need for this story.

## Now try these

1. Choose one of your favourite stories and write the plot in a diagram like *Daedelus and Icarus*. Think of what happens in the beginning, the middle and the end of the story.
    Use arrows to join the parts of the story together.
2. Choose one of these story titles and write the plot in a diagram like *Daedelus and Icarus*.
    a) The magic gate
    b) The gentle giant
    c) How the beetle helped the elephant

# Characters in stories

This is a story from the New Testament about a father's great love for his foolish son. It shows you how to describe characters. It also shows how a story can teach a lesson in an interesting way.

There once lived a farmer who had two sons. The elder son was a great help to him, but the younger son was discontented. He didn't like animals and hated farm work. He dreamed of going away and finally asked his father for his share of the farm. Then he sold this for money and went away.

> The setting shows the son is selfish

The son enjoyed himself for a while, giving wild parties and taking everyone to restaurants and clubs. In this way, he had plenty of friends around him.

> He behaves badly

Then one day his money ran out. He had spent it all. Now that he was poor, his false friends left him. He had to go to work on a pig farm and nearly starved because the pig farmer would not give him any food.

> He finds he has no friends

He remembered how kind his father had been to his servants and wished he had not left home. So he decided to return home and ask his father to forgive him. "Will my father take me back?" he wondered. "I'm not good enough to be his son."

He didn't know that his father had missed him and wanted him to come back. Thin and ragged, the son nearly fell into his father's arms when they saw each other. His father hugged and kissed him.

That was not all. His father dressed him in fine clothes and jewellery and celebrated his return with a huge party. The older son asked his father why his brother deserved such a welcome. His father replied: "A father's great love never dies, even for a foolish son."

> He realises he has been foolish

> His father shows great love

## Think about it

1. How do we know the boy was foolish?
2. How do we know the boy's friends were false?
3. How do we know the boy had learnt his lesson?
4. What lesson do you think the story teaches us?
5. Do you think the boy deserved his father's love?

## Now try these

1. Imagine you are a worker on the first farm in the story. Write a letter to a friend describing the younger son's character at the beginning of the story.
2. Write your own story to teach one of these lessons:
   a) not to be greedy
   b) not to get someone into trouble
   c) not to lie.

# Continuing a story

This traditional story of King Arthur ends with him becoming king. You will have the chance to write what happens after that.

| Usual traditional tale opening |
|---|

| Magic often in story |
|---|

| True parents may be unknown |
|---|

| Hero may have to pass hard test |
|---|

Long ago King Uther Pendragon and his wife Igraine ruled England.

One day Merlin visited the king. Merlin was a magician and often used his magic powers to give advice to the king. This time, Merlin told the king that Igraine was going to give birth to a son who was going to be a great man. Merlin also told the king that his son would be in danger from the moment he was born, so he must be hidden away safely. A knight called Sir Ector would look after him. The boy was called Arthur. He was brought up by Sir Ector and his wife as their own son.

When Arthur was still quite young, he was taken by Sir Ector to a great tournament. All the lords and knights of Britain were there. Outside of the Great Church they saw a strange sight. There was a huge stone, and in the stone was stuck a beautiful sword. On the stone was written:

Whoever can pull this sword out of the stone is the true King of England.

All the knights tried to pull the sword from the stone but all failed.

The next day, a knight called Sir Kay was fighting in the tournament but he had forgotten his sword. He asked Arthur to go and fetch it for him. Arthur passed the piece of stone and thought it would save time if he took the sword from there instead of going all the way back to Sir Kay's lodgings. He pulled the sword out easily and took it to Sir Kay.

When the knights saw that Arthur had taken the sword from the stone, they were amazed. Sir Ector told Arthur that he was the son of the dead king, Uther Pendragon. Arthur then became King of England.

Ending usually happy

## Think about it

1. Make a diagram to show the plot of the story.
   Remember to mark it 'beginning', 'middle' and 'end'.
   Join the different parts of the story with arrows.
2. Imagine you are Sir Kay.
   Arthur brings you the sword.
   You know it is the one from the stone.
   Write the conversation you have with Arthur.

## Now try these

Write a different ending for the story so that:

a) One of the other knights pulls the sword out of the stone.
   What happens?

   **or**

b) Arthur pulls the sword out of the stone but the other knights do not want him to be king.
   What happens?

# Poetry

This poem gives you a good idea of how to use rhyming words in poetry. It also has a rhythm (beat) that makes it fun to read aloud.

Same lines again (second and fifteenth)

Same words again

Rhyming words at the end of lines

Rhyming words in the same line

It's full of the moon
The dogs dance out
Through brush and bush and bramble.
They howl and yowl
And growl and prowl.
They amble ramble scramble.
They rush through brush.
The push through bush.
The yip and yap and hurr.
They lark around and bark around
With prickles in their fur.
They two-step in the meadow.
They polka on the lawn.
Tonight's the night
the dogs dance out
And chase their tails till dawn.

**Karla Kuskin**

# Think about it

1. In your own words, write what the poem is about.
2. Copy and complete the chart by finding the rhyming words in the poem.
3. Then add two more of your own rhyming words to each list.

| hurr | lawn | lark | howl | bramble | brush |
|------|------|------|------|---------|-------|
|      |      |      |      |         |       |
|      |      |      |      |         |       |
|      |      |      |      |         |       |
|      |      |      |      |         |       |
|      |      |      |      |         |       |

# Now try these

Copy out the first six lines of the poem and add
different rhyming words of your own.

It's full of the moon
The dog's dance out
Through _____ and _____ and _____.
They _____ and _____
And _____ and _____
They _____ _____ _____.

Can you do the same thing with
the rest of the poem?

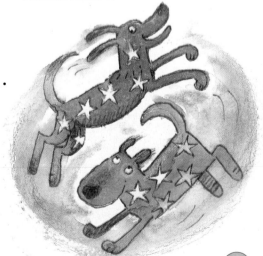

# Instructions

Here are the instructions for playing Snakes and Ladders. You will see that you have to tell the players everything they need to know.

Short description of the game

## Object of the game
The object of the game is to get to the last square before the other players.

How many can play

## Number of players
The game is best played with 2 to 4 players.

What you need

## Equipment
You will need:
– a Snakes and Ladders board
– a dice and shaker
– a counter for each player

Step by step instructions

## How to play
1. Each player takes it in turn to throw the dice.
2. A player must throw a 6 before she or he can start.
3. If a 6 is thrown, the player has a second throw.
4. Each player moves a counter the number of squares shown by the number on the dice.
5. If the counter lands on the foot of a ladder, it is moved up the ladder. But if the counter lands on the head of a snake, it has to slide down the snake.

# Think about it

Imagine that a spaceship has just landed from Planet Flippy. Use these headings to write instructions to teach the Flippy people how to play your favourite game.

**Object of the game**
**Number of players**
**Equipment**
    You will need:
**How to play**
**A plan of the field** (if you choose football or rounders and think this will help to make the instructions clearer)

# Now try these

Sometimes we need to write instructions for other things.
Imagine that the Zippy people have asked you how to make sandwiches.
Think about the type of sandwich you will write instructions for, then write:

**The type of sandwich**
**The ingredients needed**
**The stages for making the sandwiches**
(The pictures below will give you a clue.)

This page from an information book shows you how to use the most important words and phrases to make your writing easy to understand. It also explains how paragraphs are used.

## PROTECTION

Introduction should be interesting and say what to expect

Key words and phrases

1.  All <u>creatures</u> need to <u>protect themselves</u>. If they can't protect themselves, they <u>might be killed</u> and <u>eaten</u> by <u>bigger or stronger</u> animals. Here are some of the ways they keep safe.
2.  Creatures like the giraffe and springbok use their speed to escape from danger. Some, like the deer and hare, can change direction suddenly if they are being chased.

Each paragraph has different information about protection

3.  Camouflage is used by many animals, birds, fish and reptiles. The picture shows how a creature's colours, pattern or shape can blend with the trees, plants or rocks around them. This makes it hard for enemies to see them.

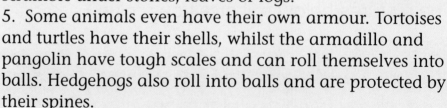

Pictures give much information too

4.  Creatures such as squirrels, moles, shrews and coral fish hide when they are frightened. They rush into holes or hide in the nearest tree. Many insects scramble under stones, leaves or logs.
5.  Some animals even have their own armour. Tortoises and turtles have their shells, whilst the armadillo and pangolin have tough scales and can roll themselves into balls. Hedgehogs also roll into balls and are protected by their spines.
6.  Large, strong animals, such as bears and tigers, protect themselves by fighting back.
7.  Some animals, such as the Portuguese man-o'-war jellyfish, keep their enemies away with poison or stings.

# Think about it

1. Look at the first paragraph. The most important words are underlined:

   1 <u>creatures</u>  <u>protect themselves</u>
   <u>might be killed</u>  <u>eaten</u>  <u>bigger or stronger</u>

   Write down the most important words in each of the other six paragraphs.

2. This chart shows ways that animals protect themselves.
   List some animals in each box.

| | |
|---|---|
| running away | |
| camouflage | |
| hiding | |
| armour | |
| fighting back | |
| poison, stings | |

# Now try these

Neatly copy these sentences.
Underline the most important words in each sentence.
a) The best camouflage colour is similar to the colours around the animal.
b) Camouflage works best if the animals keep very still and look like parts of the plants on which they are sitting.
c) Humans are the animals who keep safe by using their brains to invent protections.

# Using key points

Sometimes it is better to use a diagram to explain something.
There are many useful diagrams and charts.
This is a flow diagram.

## The seasons of the year

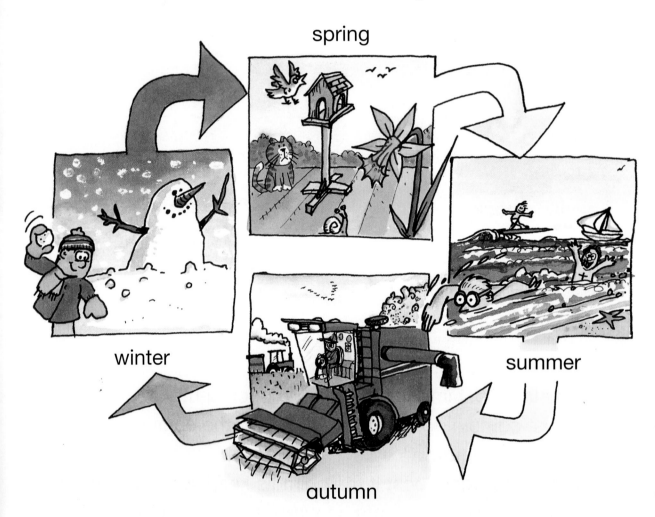

spring

winter

summer

autumn

This is called a flow diagram because information in one
picture moves along easily, or 'flows', into the next picture.

## Think about it

1. Look at the flow diagram of the seasons.
   Answer these questions.
   a) Which season comes after winter?
   b) In which season are most crops harvested?
   c) In which season do we have snow?
   d) In which season are we most likely to swim in the sea?
2. Draw four boxes. In each box write the name of the season and something you like to do in that season.

## Now try these

Write a list of the main things that you do on each school day. Then make a flow diagram of the main activities.
(You won't be able to put everything in your diagram.)
Start at the time you wake in the morning and finish when you go to bed.
Your diagram might look like this:

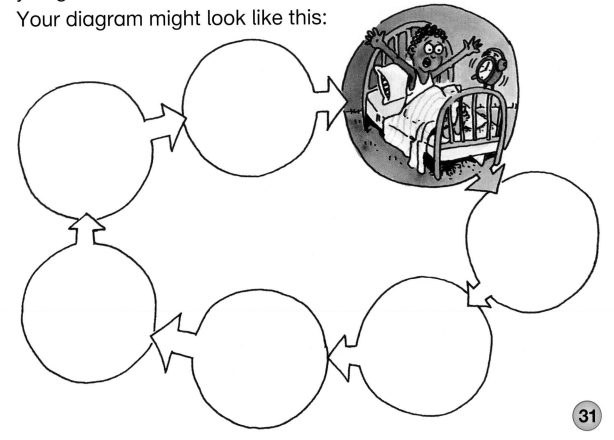

# How stories make you feel

This story is written in a way to make you feel like the characters feel. It also describes the things that make them and you feel like this.

*Joe and his sister Minna have gone to stay with their Granny. In the garden next door there is an old tree that hangs over into Granny's garden. Granny is very fond of the tree and calls it the owl tree.*

*One day, Granny is very upset because the man next door is going to have the owl tree chopped down. The children think he is a monster, but Joe decides to visit him and try to persuade him to leave the tree alone.*

He chose late afternoon. It would be almost dark, yet clear enough for him to see his way up to the monster's door.

> This makes the mood mysterious and frightening

And if he stayed outside in the dusky garden, maybe the monster wouldn't see him properly, and the ugly face wouldn't seem so frightening.

> Helps explain why Joe is so nervous

Granny Diamond had fallen asleep by the fire when Joe slipped out of the house. Minna was upstairs listening to music. Joe closed the front door quietly and walked down to the gate. Clouds of leaves spiralled from the rowan tree and the brown, velvety ground deadened his footsteps. He reached the monster's gate and took a deep breath of autumn air, hoping it was full of courage. And then he was on the neat stone path that led to the monster's door.

> Inside the house everything is warm and cosy

> Joe needs courage because he is not feeling brave

Joe found himself facing a brass knocker in the shape of a lion's head. He couldn't touch it. He stepped back and scanned the windows. The house

> This could be scary too

was in darkness, its owner asleep, perhaps. How could Joe rouse a sleeping monster? The rage would be terrible.

But he wouldn't give up, not yet. He crept round to the side of the house where a strip of light shone from a window. Joe moved closer to the source of light and peered through a gap between two heavy curtains. Soon his face was almost touching the glass pane, and the details of the room beyond swam into focus.

Makes the reader feel frightened for Joe

This tells us Joe is trying not to make a noise

**from *The Owl Tree* by Jenny Nimmo**

## Think about it

1. Imagine you are Joe and you are making your way to the 'monster's' house. Describe how you would feel.
2. Imagine the 'monster' was a lonely old man who was really very kind. Describe the room you think Joe would have seen through the curtains.
3. Suppose Joe did knock at the door and the 'monster' opened it. Write what Joe might say to persuade him to leave the owl tree alone.

## Now try these

Imagine you are going to write a story where one of the characters gets caught in a very bad storm.
Write the part of the story where it begins to rain so that your reader will:
a) be frightened  **or**  b) be amused
**or**  c) feel sorry for your character.

# Writing about myself

When you use 'I' in a story, you are writing in the first person.
You write about your own experiences in this way.

Looking back
and
remembering

Describing the
setting

Remembering
some of the
people

When I was a small child, I spent my summers in
Stainbrig with my Grannie Ellen. It is far to the west and
north of here; a long day's journey by
train, then bus and then a hired
donkey-cart. When you get near to it,
you can see mountains curving away
in great high peaks behind the little harbour. A narrow
sea loch splits the town in two, and there is a low stone
bridge across it.

Remembering
the journey

On one side the land is flat, and the houses crouch
behind the sea wall with their backs to the water.
The harbour folk are mostly fishermen, but they hardly
catch anything. They won't put to sea when the wind
stirs the waves to foam, or the soft grey haar creeps over
the water. When they do go out, they stay close to the
shore, and keep well away from the deeps.

"Are they afraid of the sea?" I asked
Grannie Ellen, and she said, "No, but
they are afraid of its mystery and magic."

Remembering
her Grannie's
words

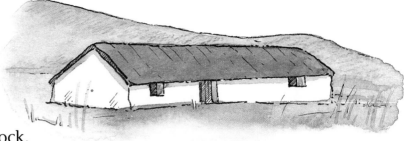

They are happier on dry land, where they grow oats and tatties and keep sheep on the sloping fields. On the far side of the loch, the land rises up in a low tummock. There is only one house there. It is a stone cottage thatched with turf, with sea on three sides of it and mountains behind. It is Tigh na eilean, where my Grannie Ellen lives.

Describing where her Grannie lives

She doesn't have much to do with the townfolk, apart from when she shops there, and she says it suits her like that. "They're a dour lot," she says, "there's no sparkle in them at all."

Some people might think there's a deal too much sparkle in my Grannie. She must be quite old, and her hair is pearl-white, but she swims in the sea every day, and goes gadding over the hills in all weathers and all season.

Describing her Grannie

**from *The Silkie* by Sandra Ann Horn**

# Think about it

1. Why do you think the writer remembers lots of detail about staying with her Grannie?
2. What does the writer remember about the harbour folk?
3. What does the writer remember about Grannie Ellen?

# Now try these

1. Think of a place that you have visited.
   It might be somewhere you have been on holiday,
   or somewhere near to where you live, like a park.
   Write a description of the place, saying why you like it
   and what you do there.
2. Choose a person you know well and write about them.
   Remember to include your own thoughts and feelings
   about them.

# Book reviews

The first book review talks mostly about the characters and what happens in the story. The second book review is different. It is more about the reasons for not liking the book.

### A Holiday Adventure

### by James Finn

**Brief telling of story**

This is a story of five children who go to stay with their uncle in Cornwall. He lives in an old cottage by the sea. The children think they will be bored and are not looking forward to going.

Once they arrive, however, they do not have a moment to be bored! Their uncle is quite an odd character who leads them into an adventure looking for the wreck of an old Spanish ship with its sunken treasure. They meet a whole host of interesting characters along the way, including Mr Berry, the innkeeper and Mrs Todd, who some of the villagers say is a witch!

**Something about characters**

**Opinion**

This book can be enjoyed by both adults and children and really makes you want to go on turning the pages to see what happens next.

## Mystery at Creek Cove

### by H. Downs

This book may be called a 'mystery' but there is really nothing mysterious about it! It is obvious almost from the first page that there is no sea monster and that Mr Cork, the bad tempered fisherman, is doing everything he can to keep people away from the cove.

Opinion

Reasons for opinion

    We never really find out why he doesn't want anyone there or why he tries so hard to convince everyone that there is a sea monster. As this is the only thing that would keep you reading – don't bother!

# Think about it

## A Holiday Adventure

1. In your own words, write what the book is about.
2. Who are the characters in the book?
3. Why doesn't the reviewer tell you what happens at the end of the book?
4. What is the reviewer's opinion of the book?
5. Would you like to read this book? Give your reasons.

## Mystery Creek

1. What is the reviewer's opinion of the book?
2. Would you like to read this book? Give your reasons.

# Now try these

1. Choose a book that you have enjoyed very much and write a book review that would make your friends want to read it.
2. Write a book review of a book that you did not enjoy and would not recommend to your friends.

# Sound poetry

This poem uses many made-up words that make you think of sounds. Some of them are very funny. They all try to help you imagine you hear what is going on.

## Muddy Boots

Trudging down the country lane,
Splodgely thlodgely plooph,
Two foot deep in slimy mud.
Faloomph Polopf Gallooph.
Hopolosplodgely go your boots,
Slopthopy grunthalamie golumph.
Then you find firm ground again,
Plonky shlonky clonky.
BUT... then you sink back in again,
Squelchy crathpally hodgle.

> Setting the scene (and line 11)

> Made-up words like sounds: lines 2, 4, 5, 6, 8, 10, 12, 14, 16, 18, 19

Sitting outside scraping your boots,
Scalpey gulapy criketty,
Cursing the horrible six inch slodge,
Scrapey flakey cakey.
Flakes of mud, crisping off the boots,
Crinkey splinky schlinkle.
Never again will I venture into that
...Schlodgely, Flopchely, Thodgely,
schrinkshely, slimy, grimy, squelchy, ghastly MUD!

**Philip Paddon**

# Think about it

1. Here are some of the real words the poet used to make up words like sounds.
   Find the matching made-up word in the poem and write it in your book.

   | splodge | plop | gallop |
   |---------|------|--------|
   | slop | grunt | plonk |
   | scrape | scalp | |

2. Make up three more words that could describe the sound of boots walking through thick mud.
3. Make up three more words that could describe the sound of boots on hard ground.

# Now try these

1. Make up a list of words that could describe the sound of:
   a) walking through leaves in autumn
   b) a washing machine
   c) someone eating crisps.
2. Use one list of words you made up to write a sound poem of your own.

# Writing a letter

This shows you how to set out a letter. It also reminds you of all the things you need to put into it.

Your address ▶ 18 River Road
New Town
Middleshire

The date ▶ Thursday 12th May

The person you're writing to ▶ Dear Granma

It has hardly stopped raining for at least a week. We have been watching the river, because the water has been rising more and more each day. Then last night it burst its banks and our road is now flooded.

The news you're giving ▶ It's very exciting. We can't get to school. The buses aren't running, and when Dad tried to drive to work his car got stuck and we all had to push him out of the water.

Our friend owns a rubber dinghy and we have been having great fun rowing up and down the road! Old Mrs Fowler had run out of bread and milk, so we took it to her in the boat. She was very pleased.

The fire engine has just arrived to pump water out of the houses and some soldiers are building a wall with sandbags to hold the water back.

We've taken some photos which we'll show you when we see you next week.

The ending ▶ Love,

Your name ▶ Rudy

# Think about it

Write a letter to someone in your family about something interesting that you have done.

Remember the five things your letter needs:

1. your address
2. the date
3. the name of the person you are writing to
4. an interesting message (the longest part)
5. your name at the end.

# Now try these

When the floods went down, Rudy went back to school. His teacher asked him to write about the flood for the school magazine. Pretend you are Rudy. Write about the flood in a way that will interest your school friends.

Use this plan:

1. what the weather was like before the flood
2. the problems the flood caused
3. who helped, and how
4. how you felt about the flood.

Think of a good headline to put at the top of your article. You might choose to draw a picture of something that you have written about.

# UNIT 20

# A news report

A newspaper story is written in a special way. It explains who the story is about, what they did, and where and when things happened. It will have a headline and the reporter's name.

A catchy headline

Name of reporter

Says who, what, where, when

More details about what happened

# RESCUED

**From Arghana Bhalla**

Annie and Tim Lindsay are heroes to 84-year-old Mrs Mandra Desai. "They saved my life," she said from her hospital bed last night.

Annie and Tim were on their way home from school when they heard cries coming from the other side of a wall. The two youngsters went into the garden to investigate and found Mrs Desai lying on the path.

Mrs Desai had fallen and broken her hip. She couldn't move. It was getting dark and beginning to rain. Annie covered the elderly woman with her coat, while Tim ran to call an ambulance.

"Without their quick-thinking and action, Mrs Desai could have been left unconscious all night," said a hospital spokesman. "That would have been very serious."

What someone else said

"I owe my life to Annie and Tim," said Mrs Desai. "As soon as I get home I shall be baking them the biggest cake they have ever had!"

# Think about it

Imagine that you are
Annie or Tim and
helped Mrs Desai.
You have been asked to
describe what happened
in the school magazine.
Make notes in your book
of a few words and
phrases that you might
use to describe each
stage of the event:

1. as you were walking home and heard the cries
2. when you went into Mrs Desai's garden
3. while you were waiting for the ambulance
4. when you visited Mrs Desai later in hospital.

# Now try these

1. Use the words and phrases that you have collected and
   write the article for your school magazine. Make up a
   good headline, too.
2. Write a letter to your grandparents telling them about what
   happened to Mrs Desai, and how you were able to help.
   Remember the five things your letter needs:
   > your address
   > the date
   > the name of the person you are writing to
   > three or four paragraphs describing what happened
   > your name at the end.

# Alphabetical order

Main words in information books can be listed by their first letters. This is called alphabetical order. It can make information easy to find.

Here is a page from a reference book about ships.

The subjects are arranged in alphabetical order.

Words listed in order of their first letter

When two words start with the same letter, the second letter is used to put the words in order

**bulk carriers**  These ships carry just one type of cargo. An oil tanker, like the one in the picture, is a bulk carrier; it only carries oil in its hold.

**container ships**  The cargo is packed into containers, that are brought to the ship on trains and lorries. The containers are all the same size and fit neatly into the ship's hold.

**cruise liners**  Most cruise liners, like the Queen Elizabeth II, are now used mainly as holiday cruise ships. They used to take passengers who wanted to travel to far-off countries.

*A hovercraft*

**ferries**  These carry people, cars and lorries from one side of a river or narrow sea to the other.

**hovercraft**  Hovercraft float on a cushion of air which is pumped into their 'skirt'.

Pictures give some more information

**steamships**  The first ships with engines rather than sails were driven by steam engines. Now most ships have diesel engines.

# Think about it

1. Answer these questions about alphabetical order.
   a) Does hockey come before or after athletics?
   b) Does football come before or after skating?
   c) Does snooker come before or after basketball?
2. Write each of these three lists in your book in alphabetical order.

| | | |
|---|---|---|
| sparrow | Germany | Edinburgh |
| robin | France | Belfast |
| blackbird | Italy | Cardiff |
| thrush | Spain | Swansea |
| finch | Belgium | Newcastle |
| jackdaw | United Kingdom | Plymouth |

# Now try these

1. Make a page for an information book, like the one about ships.
   Set the information out in alphabetical order.
   Make it about something you are interested in,
   like your family, **or** birds **or** football teams.
   Think about:
   – where you can find the information you will need
   – how many subjects you can get on one page
   – how you will set out the page to make it look good.
2. Write the words in each of these groups in the order you would find them in a dictionary.
   a) ant   apple   aircraft   actor   adder
   b) chair   cloth   cup   circle   cat
   c) packet   please   putter   pool   pram

# UNIT 22 Paragraphs

It is hard to read a big block of writing. Paragraphs break up the big block into smaller blocks that are easier to read. Most paragraphs have two or more sentences in them.

## Dogs as pets

Keeping a dog is a big responsibility.

There are many <u>different kinds</u> of dogs; some are kept only as <u>pets</u>, but some do important <u>work</u>, such as police dogs, guide dogs, sniffer dogs and sheep dogs.

All dogs need company and exercise. Bigger dogs, such as Alsatians and Great Danes, need much more exercise than smaller dogs like Chihuahuas and Yorkshire Terriers. Dogs need exercise every day. They should be taken for a walk on a lead, until they are in an area where it is free from traffic and safe. Then they can be let off the lead.

Key words and phrases

Paragraph about exercise

Wild dogs, such as foxes and wolves, hunt other animals for food. Tame dogs like to eat meat too, so dogs can be expensive pets to keep. Some vets say that about half the food a dog eats should be meat. The other half should be bread or cereal and dog biscuits. A full-grown dog needs one meal a day, and should always have a bowl of fresh water to drink. Dogs enjoy gnawing large bones, but should never be given bones that crack and splinter, like chicken bones.

*Paragraph about food*

A dog can sleep outdoors in a kennel, provided it is dry and large enough for the dog to move around. Straw makes good bedding, but it should be changed each week. If your dog is kept indoors in a dog basket, it should have a blanket that is washed whenever it is dirty.

*Paragraph about sleeping*

Dogs should be brushed each day and given a bath regularly with warm water and dog soap. Sometimes they may need to be sprayed to kill any fleas. All dogs need to be taken to the vet for regular injections to protect them against certain dog illnesses.

*Paragraph about bathing and health*

If you can do all these things, and your home is big enough for a dog, then you will be a good owner and you will have a happy and contented pet.

*Conclusion*

## Think about it

1. Name four types of work that dogs can do.
2. Make a list of the things dogs need to eat and drink.
3. Where can dogs sleep?
4. How should you keep your dog clean?
5. Why do dogs need to be taken to a vet regularly?

## Now try these

1. Look at the first paragraph. The most important words are underlined:

   different kinds    pets    work

   Write down the most important words in each of the other paragraphs.
2. Use the words you have written in question 1 to help you write a much shorter version of 'Dogs as pets'.
   Use no more than five sentences, but be careful to include all the most important information.
3. Find another information book that interests you.
   Try to write a shorter version of a page from that book.
   Be sure to include all the most important information.